30 Easily Taught Bible Doctrines

Foreword by
KEN HAM

GOD is
REALLY, REALLY
REAL

by Jeff
Davenport

First printing: October 2015
Second printing: July 2019

New Leaf Press is a division of the
New Leaf Publishing Group, Inc.

ISBN: 978-0-89221-738-0
ISBN: 978-1-61458-458-2 (digital)
Library of Congress Number: 2015945009

Unless otherwise noted, Scripture quotations are
from the English Standard Version of the Bible.

Please consider requesting that a copy of this
volume be purchased by your local library system.

Printed in China

Please visit our website for other great titles:
www.newleafpress.com

For information regarding author
interviews, please contact the publicity
department at (870) 438-5288.

01.

A Brightly-Illustrated & Rhyming Account of Scripture

Enjoy a quick overview of biblical history
from Creation to Christ in the form of fun,
rhyming verses you can read each week.
God is Really, Really Real is designed to
help teach children 30 essential biblical
doctrines in a creative yet effective way.
As children interact with both the picture
book and doctrines, they will become
better equipped to understand and
confront future doubts and challenges to
their faith.

Depending on the developmental age
of each child, you can use all or some of
these helps to communicate the individual
truths.

02.

30 Essential Biblical Truths & Tuck-In Questions

Each of the 30 biblical lessons begin with a core concept and its importance; then a short verse and an informational paragraph follows.

- With younger children, it might be a good idea to begin by just talking about a specific doctrine heading such as, "What are some things that God created?"

- For older children, you can read, discuss, and memorize each statement and its meaning such as, "God has always been alive, and He created everything!"

Perfect to personalize for your child, you can use as much or as little of the included information that you feel is needed for your child's understanding. There are two Tuck-In questions included and space to add one of your own!

03.

Helpful Text for Parents

In the Additional Helps section at the end of the book, you will find extra thoughts and Scriptures for each doctrine. This section is designed to help you dig deeper into God's Word as you prepare to speak to your child and also to help answer some of the questions they may ask you.

Foreword
A NOTE TO PARENTS

Many parents think that just reading an account from the Bible to their children as a bedtime "story" is teaching them God's Word. However, children need not only to know what God's Word says, but also to understand the depth of the content, the doctrines that come out of it, and how to apply it to their lives.

From conception, all of us have a sin nature that is not desirous of God's Word. The devil can so easily use this sin nature to drag these dear ones the Lord has entrusted to us away from God's Word. The broad way with its secular education system, media, evolutionary museums, entertainment, and other resources is having catastrophic influences on the coming generations.

That's why parents need to be so diligent in teaching their children to acquire a taste for the things of the Lord, basically from when they are born. In our modern world, it seems many Christian materials have watered down the teaching of God's Word to the extent that much of it these days is what I call "fluff and stuff." Children have an innate God-given incredible ability to learn and comprehend complex matters.

That's why I love this new book for children entitled *God Is Really, Really Real*. This is an exciting opportunity for parents to teach their children God's Word and delve into the richness of the content in a way they will remember. Yes, God is really, really real, and parents have a God-commanded responsibility to ensure children are taught the wonderful truths God gives us — and teach them in a way that they will understand and remember. That's what *God Is Really, Really Real* is all about.

—Ken Ham
President Answers in Genesis,
Creation Museum,
and Ark Encounter

WELCOME!

The fact that you are reading these words probably means you have a child or children in your life that you care a lot about. Like me, you want them to understand who God is and the unique plan He has for them. That unique plan is found in the Bible!

God Is Really, Really Real is designed to help teach children 30 essential biblical doctrines in a creative yet effective way. As children interact with both the picture book and doctrines, they will become better equipped to understand and confront future doubts and challenges to their faith. Much research has proven that we are losing our children while they are still young! One survey reported, "Three out of every five young Christians (59%) disconnect either permanently or for an extended period of time from church life after age 15." That's alarming! However, I am confident that *God Is Really, Really Real* will help young people better understand what they believe so they will not so easily be persuaded to walk away from their faith.

As you guide your children in establishing a foundation of biblical truth, you will help them on their way to understanding all that God has in store for them as He reveals it in His Word! *God Is Really, Really Real* will help plant biblical truth into the minds of children, while prayerfully awaiting the day God reveals it to their hearts!

— Jeff Davenport

This book is lovingly dedicated to my precious grandchildren, whom I love deeply and whom God amazingly loves even more!

It's so much fun to learn about God,
Like how He created the clouds and the sod
And then turned some sod into a man,
But didn't stop there with His master plan.

He made a woman from the rib of that guy,
And gave them a garden with a pretty blue sky.
He gave them the earth and He gave it for free,
Except for the fruit on this one special tree.

God told them, "Don't eat it or else you will die."
They both said, "Okay" and didn't ask why.
They trusted in God and were having a blast!
They did what He asked, but that didn't last.

Along came Satan disguised as a snake,
He held out some fruit for the woman to take.
Adam ate the fruit after God said he shouldn't,
After Adam and Eve both said they wouldn't.

Now they felt naked in front of the Lord,
They looked for some clothes, a leaf or a gourd.
But God killed a beast and gave them its skin,
The start of His plan to cover their sin.

Because they had sinned, God kicked them right out,
They lost all their pets and lost all their clout.
Their sin broke the friendship they once had with God,
And now life was hard, and felt rather odd.

Things didn't improve; in fact it got worse.
God's perfect creation was under sin's curse.
Everything good had now turned to bad.
God would judge all, and that would be sad.

God flooded the earth and brought devastation,
But in Noah's Ark He provided salvation.
Two of each kind and Noah's whole crew,
Waited inside till God made things new.

A dove brought the news the rain had subsided,
And high on a mountain the Ark now resided.
God sent Noah to start a new life,
The animals, his kids, and also his wife.

So they tried real hard to make up for the past.
They brought God some gifts, but that didn't last.
They just could not work enough to be good,
They tried and they tried, they did all they could.

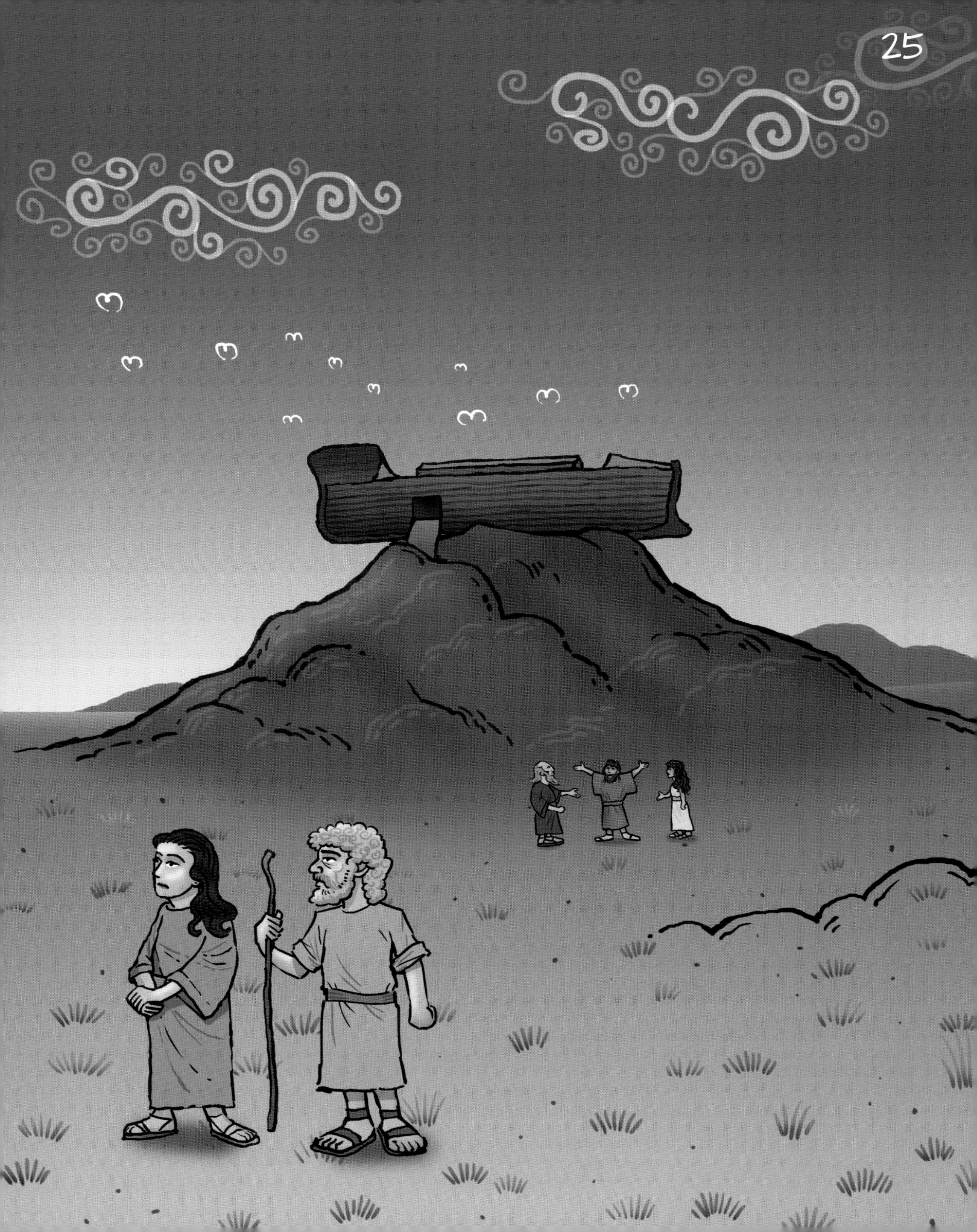

But only God knew what had to be done;
To pay for their sin, it would take His own Son.
And although it hurt, His Son came to earth,
Not as some thought, but a baby by birth.

His name was Jesus, the King of the Jews.
He came to the earth to bring the good news.
The good news is this; man's sin is forgiven.
Through Jesus alone we can now go to Heaven.

On Calvary's Cross Jesus Christ took our place,
They treated Him badly and spat in His face.
He died there for us and paid for our sin,
He said it was finished, and that was the end.

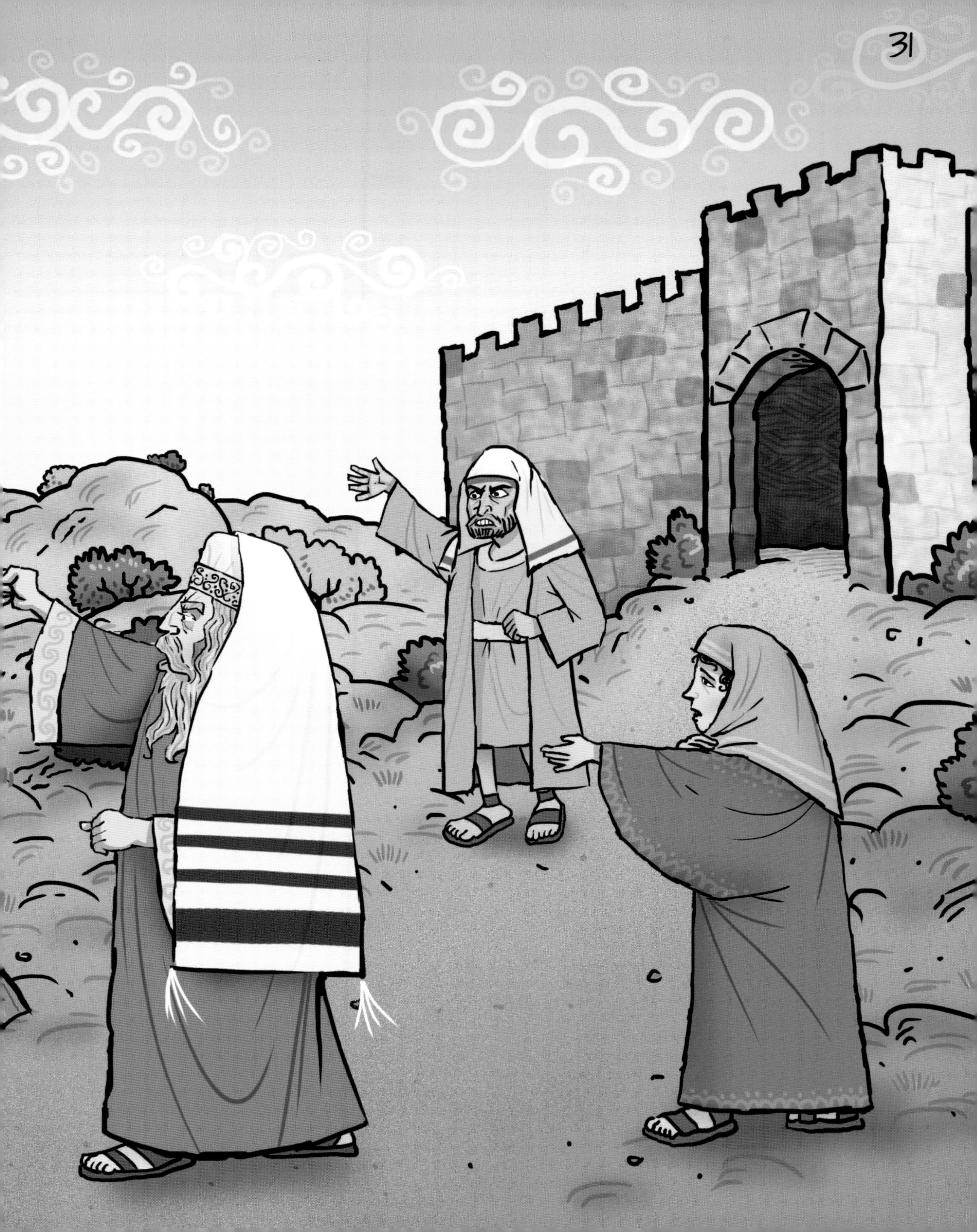

After He died, in a grave He was laid.
It seemed God had lost, hope started to fade.
But on the third day, up He arose!
Sin and death were defeated, God conquered His foes!

Now we can pray and ask God to forgive,
And one day He'll take us to Heaven to live.
The next thing that happens, I'm so sad to tell,
Those people who don't - live forever in Hell.

But those who got saved, God gave them His Word,
And sent them to tell so everyone heard.
Salvation is free, put a smile on your face,
It won't cost you a thing; it's given by grace.

So people got saved and got a new start.
God gave them His Spirit to live in their hearts.
Their sins were forgiven; they didn't feel odd.
The best thing of all, they were now friends with God.

God formed them a group and called it a church.
They preached and prayed and started to search.
They wanted to find the ones who were lost;
They promised to do it no matter the cost.

They baptized each one and got them all wet.
They all took communion so they wouldn't forget.
They never forgot what God promised to do;
One day He would come back for me and for you.

Until God comes back, we must learn all we can.
We must study His Word and follow His plan.
He's written it down in His one perfect book,
So open a Bible and let's take a look.

I think you will like the words that you read;
They get in your heart and grow like a seed.
They help you to do and say what is right;
They help you to live by faith and not sight.

Faith helps us to trust what God said is true,
And all that He said, one day He will do.
The time has now come; let's all seal the deal;
There's no doubt about it, God is Really, Really REAL!

Lesson 1

ABOUT GOD

God created everything and is ruler over all.

"Worthy are you, our Lord and God, to receive glory and honor and power, for you created all things, and by your will they existed and were created."

—Revelation 4:11

God has always existed. God has no beginning and no end; He is eternal. God is perfect, He knows all things, He has the power to do all things, and He loves unselfishly. God is the Creator, and He created everything in the heavens and on the earth for His glory. Nothing happened by accident; God designed it all, and He is the Supreme Ruler over all creation. No person is greater than God.

TUCK-IN QUESTIONS

1. Who created everything?

2. Why did God create everything?

3. _____?

Additional Helps (About God) on page 80

Lesson 2

ABOUT THE TRINITY
The Trinity is God the Father, Son, and Holy Spirit.

"Go therefore and make disciples of all nations, baptizing them in the name of the Father and of the Son and of the Holy Spirit."

—Matthew 28:19

The word "trinity" means three. There is only one God, but that one God exists as three individual persons. Those three persons are the Father, the Son, and the Holy Spirit. All three are equally God. Each person of the Trinity is separate, yet they make up one eternal God. God is not complete without all three persons of the Trinity. Although there are three persons, we worship them as one complete God.

TUCK-IN QUESTIONS

1. What number do you think of when I say Trinity?

2. Can you name the three persons in God's Trinity?

3. _____?

Additional Helps (About the Trinity) on page 80

Lesson 3

ABOUT CREATION
God created everything in six real days.

"In the beginning, God created the heavens and the earth."

—Genesis 1:1

God is the Creator. He created everything. The Bible tells us that God created the heavens and the earth, the darkness and light, the sky, water, land, plants, trees, sun, moon, stars, fish, birds, animals, and man in six, 24-hour days. The Hebrew word in the Bible for "day" does not mean millions and millions of years; it means one, 24-hour day. After God had finished creating everything in six days, He rested on the seventh day because creation was complete.

TUCK-IN QUESTIONS

1. How many days did it take God to create everything?

2. How many hours are in one day?

3. _____?

Additional Helps (About Creation) on page 81

Lesson 4

ABOUT MANKIND
God created us in His image.

"So God created man in his own image, in the image of God he created him; male and female he created them."

—Genesis 1:27

God created us in His own image. Like God, we have intelligence and the ability to love. God is perfect in His intelligence and love. Sin limits our intelligence and capacity to love. God created each one of us on purpose. None of us is an accident, but instead, we are wonderful creations by God, lovingly designed and created for a unique purpose. Although God knows we are not perfect, He expects us to be growing to become more like His Son, Jesus.

TUCK-IN QUESTIONS

1. Who created man and woman?

2. Who were we created to be like?

3. _____?

Additional Helps (About Mankind) on page 81

Lesson 5

ABOUT MARRIAGE

God created marriage between one man and one woman.

"Therefore a man shall leave his father and his mother and hold fast to his wife, and they shall become one flesh."

—Genesis 2:24

God made man from dust of the ground. God did not want man to be alone, so He created woman. God also created marriage for the man and woman so they could live together as a family and have children. God created marriage to be between one man and one woman, for life.

TUCK-IN QUESTIONS

1. Who created marriage?

2. Why did God create the first woman?

3. _____?

Additional Helps (About Marriage) on page 81

Lesson 6

ABOUT HOLINESS

God is holy, and everything He does is perfect.

"For I am the LORD your God. Consecrate yourselves therefore, and be holy, for I am holy…"

—Leviticus 11:44

God is holy; He is without sin. Everything God created was perfect, but Adam brought sin to all of mankind by disobeying God. The Bible tells us that all of us sin. Our sin separates us from God because God is holy and cannot look at sin. Jesus Christ died for our sins, and through Him we can be forgiven of our sins and have friendship with God, who is holy.

TUCK-IN QUESTIONS

1. What caused man to become unholy?

2. Who was the only man who ever lived a holy life?

3. _____?

Additional Helps (About Holiness) on page 82

Lesson 7

ABOUT SATAN
Satan is God's enemy and our enemy.

"Be sober-minded; be watchful. Your adversary the devil prowls around like a roaring lion, seeking someone to devour."

—1 Peter 5:8

Satan (also called the devil and Lucifer) was an angel created by God. Satan became proud and sinned against God, so God kicked Satan out of Heaven and he fell to the earth. Now he tries to convince people to sin against God. God is greater than Satan, and one day God will cast him into Hell.

TUCK-IN QUESTIONS

1. Why did God kick Satan out of Heaven?

2. Who is greater, God or Satan?

3. _____?

Additional Helps (About Satan) on page 82

Lesson 8

ABOUT SIN

Sin is disobeying God's perfect Law.

"Therefore, just as sin came into the world through one man, and death through sin, and so death spread to all men because all sinned."

—Romans 5:12

Sin came into the perfect world God had created through the sin of Adam. Sin is anything that does not please God or that breaks one of His laws. We have all broken God's perfect law by sinning. Sin separates us from God and leads to death. Sin brought the Curse of death, disease, and destruction into God's perfect creation. Jesus Christ died for our sins, and through Him we can be forgiven of our sins.

TUCK-IN QUESTIONS

1. Who paid for our sin?

2. What are some examples of sin?

3. _____?

Additional Helps (About Sin) on page 83

Lesson 9

ABOUT JUDGMENT
God must judge sin.

"So then each of us will give an account of himself to God."

—Romans 14:12

Judgment is the ability to determine what is right and wrong. Because God is just and righteous, He must punish sin. Because God is perfect and holy, He alone has the authority to judge us. We have broken God's perfect law, as reflected in the Ten Commandments, and we deserve to be punished. But Jesus died for our sins, and through Him we can be forgiven of our sins.

TUCK-IN QUESTIONS

1. What does the word "judgment" mean?

2. How do you think God feels about our sin?

3. _____?

Additional Helps (About Judgment) on page 83

Lesson 10

ABOUT PUNISHMENT
God must punish sin.

"For the wages of sin is death, but the free gift of God is eternal life in Christ Jesus our Lord."

—Romans 6:23

Punishment is what we deserve when we do something wrong. The Bible tells us that every person has sinned and that the punishment for sin is death. The punishment we receive for our sin is eternal death, separation from God in Hell. However, Jesus Christ took the punishment for our sins when He died on the Cross. He took our place! Through Jesus Christ we can have our sins forgiven and God will not punish us.

TUCK-IN QUESTIONS

1. What does the word "punishment" mean?

2. How can we avoid being punished for our sins?

3. _____?

Additional Helps (About Punishment) on page 83

Lesson 11

ABOUT FORGIVENESS

Forgiveness is when God releases us from the punishment of our sins.

"If we confess our sins, he is faithful and just to forgive us our sins and to cleanse us from all unrighteousness."

—1 John 1:9

Forgiveness means to release someone from what they deserve. In our case, we sinned against God. God has every right to punish us for our sins because He is our Creator, but through His Son, Jesus Christ, He offers us forgiveness. Only God can forgive our sins because it is His perfect law that we have broken. God never excuses the penalty of our sin; sin must always be punished. Jesus Christ took the punishment for our sin when He shed His perfect (without sin) blood on the Cross. We must realize that we are in need of forgiveness, confess our sins to God, accept God's free gift of forgiveness, and trust in Jesus Christ as our Lord and Savior to be saved.

TUCK-IN QUESTIONS

1. Who can forgive sin?

2. Who died for our sin?

3. _____?

Additional Helps (About Forgiveness) on page 84

Lesson 12

ABOUT THE FLOOD
God judged sin with a worldwide flood.

"By faith Noah, being warned by God concerning events as yet unseen, in reverent fear constructed an ark for the saving of his household. By this he condemned the world and became an heir of the righteousness that comes by faith."

—Hebrews 11:7

The Bible tells us that because man's wickedness had become so great and there was so much sin on earth, God was grieved in His spirit (very sad) and decided He would destroy mankind with a worldwide flood. Before God flooded the earth, He led Noah to build an Ark. Noah's family and two of every kind of land creature (and seven of some) found safety behind the door of the Ark. After 40 days and nights of rain and many more days of flooding, the water level went down and the Ark finally rested safely on a mountain. Noah and his family left the Ark and started a new life.

TUCK-IN QUESTIONS

1. Why did God cause a worldwide flood?

2. How were Noah and his family saved?

3. _____?

Additional Helps (About the Flood) on page 85

Lesson 13

ABOUT PEOPLE GROUPS AND LANGUAGES

God created different people groups and languages.

"Therefore its name was called Babel, because there the LORD confused the language of all the earth. And from there the LORD dispersed them over the face of all the earth."

—Genesis 11:9

There is only one race of people, the human race. Adam and Eve were the first two people that God created and the first married couple who ever lived on earth. Everyone who has ever lived is related to Adam and Eve. Although we are all different, we all come from Adam's bloodline. After the Flood, everyone on earth spoke the same language, and God told mankind to multiply and fill the earth. Instead, they rebelled and built a city and a large tower to demonstrate their own greatness. In judgment, God confused their languages and scattered them into different groups all over the earth. That is how people groups began.

TUCK-IN QUESTIONS

1. How many races of people are there?

2. Who was the very first created human couple?

3. _____?

Additional Helps (About People Groups and Languages) on page 85

Lesson 14

ABOUT GOOD WORKS

We cannot pay for our sins with good works.

"He [God] saved us, not because of works done by us in righteousness, but according to his own mercy."

—Titus 3:5

Many people think that if they are good enough, they will go to Heaven. But God's requirement to get into Heaven is not being good, it is being perfect, without sin, which none of us are. We cannot pay for our sin by doing good works. Because we have sinned, even our good works are tainted with sin. Jesus Christ died for our sins and offers us forgiveness so that we can go to Heaven when we die. We are not saved by our good works, but we were created to do good works in order to bring glory to God.

TUCK-IN QUESTIONS

1. Can our good works pay for our sins?

2. What are our good works supposed to do?

3. _____?

Additional Helps (About Good Works) on page 86

Lesson 15

ABOUT GRACE

Grace is God giving us what we do not deserve.

"For by grace you have been saved through faith. And this is not your own doing; it is the gift of God."

—Ephesisans 2:8

We do not deserve to receive the gift of salvation from God. Because of our sin, we deserve to be punished by being eternally separated from God when we die. But God loved us so much that He sent His Son, Jesus, to die for our sins. If we ask Jesus to forgive us of our sins and to trust Him as our Lord and Savior, not only do we become a part of God's family, but we will also spend forever with Him in Heaven when we die.

TUCK-IN QUESTIONS

1. What is a gift you received just because someone loved you?

2. What is the grace gift Jesus Christ offers to us?

3. _____?

Additional Helps (About Grace) on page 86

Lesson 16

ABOUT JESUS CHRIST
Jesus is the Son of God.

"And the angel answered her, 'The Holy Spirit will come upon you, and the power of the Most High will overshadow you; therefore the child to be born will be called holy — the Son of God.'"

—Luke 1:35

Jesus Christ is God the Son. He is the second person in the Holy Trinity. Jesus left Heaven and came to earth as a baby. Jesus grew and became a man. He was God and man at the same time. Jesus came to earth to die for sinners. Jesus lived a sinless life. Although He was tempted just like us, Jesus Christ willingly laid down His life to pay for our sins. Because Jesus was a man, He could die for us. Because Jesus was God, He could pay for our sins.

TUCK-IN QUESTIONS

1. Why is it important that Jesus became a man?

2. Why is it important that Jesus is God?

3. _____?

Additional Helps (About Jesus) on page 87

Lesson 17

ABOUT THE RESURRECTION

Jesus Christ arose from the grave on the third day.

". . . that he was buried, that he was raised on the third day in accordance with the Scriptures."

—1 Corinthians 15:4

After Jesus died on the Cross, He was buried, but on the third day, He resurrected, which means He arose from the dead and became alive again. There were many people who saw Jesus after He was raised from the dead. The fact that Jesus Christ arose from the dead is very important; it proves that God has power over death. Jesus' Resurrection also proves that God the Father accepted the sacrifice of God the Son (Jesus) for sin.

TUCK-IN QUESTIONS

1. What happens when someone is resurrected?

2. Why is it important that Jesus resurrected?

3. _____?

Additional Helps (About the Resurrection) on page 87

Lesson 18

ABOUT SALVATION

Salvation is God's free gift of eternal life.

"For 'everyone who calls on the name of the Lord will be saved.'"

—Romans 10:13

Salvation is being saved from the punishment we deserve because we have sinned. We cannot save ourselves. We need someone to save us; we need a Savior. Jesus Christ came to earth to die for our sins, but we must receive His free gift of salvation by confessing our sins, asking Jesus to forgive us of our sins, and trusting in Him as our Lord and Savior.

TUCK-IN QUESTIONS

1. Can our good works save us?

2. What must we do to be saved?

3. _____?

Additional Helps (About Salvation) on page 88

Lesson 19

ABOUT HELL

Hell is a place God created to punish Satan and sinners.

"Then he will say to those on his left, 'Depart from me, you cursed, into the eternal fire prepared for the devil and his angels.'"

—Matthew 25:41

Hell is a real place, created to punish Satan and his demons. The Bible describes Hell as a lake of fire and a place of eternal (forever) punishment. Those who die without asking Jesus to forgive their sins and trusting Him as their Lord and Savior will also spend eternity in the torment of Hell forever and ever. The good news is that God loves us so much, that He made a way for us to avoid going to Hell through the forgiveness of our sins.

TUCK-IN QUESTIONS

1. Who goes to Hell when they die?

2. Why should Christians not fear Hell?

3. _____?

Additional Helps (About Hell) on page 89

Lesson 20

ABOUT THE BIBLE
The Bible is God's Word to mankind.

"All Scripture is breathed out by God and profitable for teaching, for reproof, for correction, and for training in righteousness."

—2 Timothy 3:16

The Bible is God's written Word to us. God has chosen to use the Bible to reveal to us who He is and what He is like. The Bible also teaches us who we are and who God wants us to be. The Bible reveals to us the Gospel of Jesus Christ, how we can have our sins forgiven and know God while we are here on earth, then live in Heaven with Him when we die.

TUCK-IN QUESTIONS

1. Who gave us the words in the Bible?

2. Why should we read the Bible?

3. _____?

Additional Helps (About the Bible) on page 89

Lesson 21

ABOUT THE HOLY SPIRIT

The Holy Spirit lives in the heart of every Christian.

". . . do you not know that your body is a temple of the Holy Spirit within you, whom you have from God?"

—1 Corinthians 6:19

When we ask Jesus Christ to forgive our sins and trust Him as our Lord and Savior, His Holy Spirit comes to live inside of us. The Holy Spirit is the third person of the Holy Trinity. He teaches us, guides us, and comforts us. As we pray and study God's Word, the Holy Spirit speaks to our hearts and minds so that we will know how to bring glory to God in everything we do.

TUCK-IN QUESTIONS

1. Where does the Holy Spirit live?

2. How does the Holy Spirit help us?

3. _____?

Additional Helps (About the Holy Spirit) on page 90

Lesson 22

ABOUT THE CHURCH
The church is made up of all of those who have received Salvation in Jesus Christ.

"And when they arrived and gathered the church together, they declared all that God had done with them…"

—Acts 14:27

When the Bible speaks of the Church, it is not talking about a building; it is talking about people. The Church is made up of people who have asked Jesus Christ to forgive their sins and trusted Him as their Lord and Savior and now have the Holy Spirit living inside of them (Christians). Jesus Christ is the Head of the Church because He died for every member. Each Church member is called to serve God in a local church community that teaches God's Word, tells others about the good news that Jesus died for their sins, helps Christians become more like Jesus Christ, and observes both baptism and communion.

TUCK-IN QUESTIONS

1. What makes someone a Church member?

2. Why should we join a local church?

3. _____?

Additional Helps (About the Church) on page 90

Lesson 23

ABOUT PRAYER

Prayer is talking to God.

"Do not be anxious about anything, but in everything by prayer and supplication with thanksgiving let your requests be made known to God."

—Philippians 4:6

God cares about everything in our life and He loves us! God invites those who have trusted in Him as Lord and Savior to come to Him in prayer. We can pray to God either aloud or silently. We should ask God for forgiveness when we do wrong, to guide us in what we should do, and to give us the strength to do what He wants us to do. We should also thank God personally for all of His goodness. God allows us to come directly to Him in prayer, through His Son, Jesus Christ.

TUCK-IN QUESTIONS

1. What is prayer?

2. Why should we pray to God?

3. _____?

Additional Helps (About Prayer) on page 91

Lesson 24

ABOUT EVANGELISM
Evangelism is telling others about Jesus Christ.

"And he said to them, 'Go into all the world and proclaim the gospel to the whole creation.'"

—Mark 16:15

God wants us to tell others about His free gift of salvation. If we do not tell others, they may never know the good news of the Gospel: that Jesus Christ died for their sins. We must share the good news with them using words and also in the way we live our lives. God calls every Christian to share the good news about Jesus Christ.

TUCK-IN QUESTIONS

1. What is the Gospel?

2. Why should we tell others about the Gospel?

3. _____?

Additional Helps (About Evangelism) on page 91

Lesson 25

ABOUT BAPTISM
Baptism is a public picture of our salvation.

"So those who received his word were baptized…"

—Acts 2:41

Baptism is an outward picture of an inward decision that people have already made in their hearts to trust Jesus Christ as their Lord and Savior. Baptism is a public demonstration of our commitment to Jesus Christ and is a beautiful picture of our salvation. When we are baptized, we identify ourselves with the death, burial, and Resurrection of Jesus Christ.

TUCK-IN QUESTIONS

1. Why do Christians get baptized?

2. What does baptism represent?

3. _____?

Additional Helps (About Baptism) on page 92

Lesson 26

ABOUT COMMUNION

Communion helps us remember what Jesus Christ did for us.

"For as often as you eat this bread and drink the cup, you proclaim the Lord's death until he comes."

—1 Corinthians 11:26

Communion or the Lord's Table, is another outward picture of an inward decision that people have already made in their hearts to trust Jesus Christ as their Lord and Savior. Every time we take Communion, we remember what Jesus Christ did for us on the Cross. The bread represents His body that was beaten and crucified. The cup reminds us of His sinless blood that was shed for our sins. Communion reminds us of God's amazing love for us.

TUCK-IN QUESTIONS

1. What does Communion help us remember?

2. What do the bread and the cup represent?

3. _____?

Additional Helps (About Communion) on page 92

Lesson 27

ABOUT THE RETURN OF CHRIST

Jesus will return and take Christians to Heaven.

"For the Lord himself shall descend from heaven with a cry of command, with the voice of an archangel, and with the sound of the trumpet of God. And the dead in Christ will rise first. Then we who are alive, who are left, will be caught up together with them in the clouds to meet the Lord in the air, and so we will always be with the Lord."

—1 Thessalonians 4:16-17

Shortly before Jesus died on the Cross, He told His disciples that He was getting ready to return to Heaven, but He would come back to get them so that they could be with Him forever. One day Jesus will return to earth and take everyone who has trusted Him as Lord and Savior, including those who have already died, to live with Him forever. Everything God promises, He does. We should expect Jesus to return soon and be ready for His return.

TUCK-IN QUESTIONS

1. Who will go to Heaven when Jesus returns to earth?

2. Why does Jesus take Christians to Heaven?

3. _____?

Additional Helps (About the Return of Christ) on page 92

Lesson 28

ABOUT LEARNING GOD'S WORD

God wants us to read and learn the Bible.

"I have stored up your word in my heart that I might not sin against you."
—Psalm 119:11

God has chosen to use His Word, the Bible, to reveal to us who He is, what He is like, who He wants us to be, and how He wants us to live. It is important for us to study the Bible and learn what it says so that we can obey God. God uses His Word to teach us and to encourage us. He also wants us to share with others what He has taught us, so they can know Him too.

TUCK-IN QUESTIONS

1. Where do we find God's Word written down?

2. Why should we study and memorize God's Word?

3. _____?

Additional Helps (About Learning God's Word) on page 93

Lesson 29

ABOUT FAITH

Faith is believing in something we cannot see or touch.

"Now faith is the assurance of things hoped for, the conviction of things not seen."
—Hebrews 11:1

Faith is believing in something we cannot see or touch. It takes faith to believe in God, who we cannot see, even though the world is full of proof that He exists. When we place our faith in Jesus Christ and His death on the Cross, He saves us from our sin. Faith allows us to trust God while we are on earth and spend forever in heaven with Him when we die.

TUCK-IN QUESTIONS

1. What is faith?

2. Why do we need faith?

3. _____?

Additional Helps (About Faith) on page 93

Lesson 30

ABOUT HEAVEN

Heaven is a perfect place where Christians will live forever with God.

"And if I go and prepare a place for you, I will come again and will take you to myself, that where I am you may be also."

—John 14:3

Heaven is a real place! Heaven is where God lives. Heaven is also where Christians, those who have asked Jesus to forgive them of their sins and have trusted Him as their Lord and Savior, will spend eternity (forever) when they die. Our eternal home will be a perfect place of beauty, where there will be no more death, sadness, crying, or pain because no sin will ever enter it.

TUCK-IN QUESTIONS

1. What are some wonderful things about Heaven?

2. Who gets to live in Heaven?

3. _____?

Additional Helps (About Heaven) on page 94

1. ABOUT GOD Teaching your children about God will help them better understand how to live for His glory with hope, courage, and confidence (Psalm 19:1). However, we must first understand that God is greater than any human. Because of God's supreme greatness, there are aspects about God that are beyond our ability to fully understand and explain (Exodus 15:11; 1 Corinthians 13:12). We will never fully understand everything about God until we get to Heaven. God is a loving God and He loves everyone (John 3:16). In fact, the Bible tells us that "God is love" (1 John 4:8). God is also holy, which means that He is without sin, He can do nothing wrong (Leviticus 19:2). The Bible tells us that God is so holy He cannot even look upon sin (Habakkuk 1:13). God is also just and righteous (Deuteronomy 32:4; Ezra 9:15), which means He always does what is right and fair. It is because God is just and righteous that He must punish sin. God is the Creator (Genesis 1), and He created everything. God Himself was not created; He has always existed. God is omniscient, which means He knows everything; He doesn't need anyone to teach Him anything (Jeremiah 23:24). God is omnipotent, which means He is all-powerful and can do anything (Luke 1:37). God is also omnipresent, which means He is all-present; He is everywhere (Proverbs 15:3). Learning more about God enables us to trust Him. Trust is important. Trust allows us to have confidence in a person. When we have confidence in someone, we do not only run to them in times of trouble, but even when we just want to spend time together (Psalm 31:1). Finally, teach your child that since God is greater than anyone or anything, we should worship and serve only Him (Matthew 4:10).

2. ABOUT THE TRINITY Teaching and explaining the Trinity to children can be challenging, but it is not impossible! The reality of the Trinity is taught in the Bible. The Trinity is one of the aspects about God that is beyond our ability to fully understand and explain. In teaching children about the Trinity, we must help them understand only what the Bible teaches on the subject. The concept of the Trinity means that there is only one God, but that one God exists as three individual persons. Those three persons are the Father, the Son, and the Holy Spirit. All three are equally God. The Father is God (Philippians 1:2; 2 Corinthians 1:3), Jesus Christ (the Son) is God (1 Corinthians 8:6), and the Holy Spirit is God (2 Corinthians 13:14; Acts 5:3–4). A good passage that shows all three persons in the Trinity is Matthew 3:13–17. The Trinity works together for our salvation. God requires that those who sin must be punished; that means all of us, because everyone sins (Romans 3:23). The punishment for sin is death and eternal separation from God (spending eternity in Hell — Romans 6:23). However, God required and provided a perfect blood sacrifice to pay for our sins so that we do not have to be separated from Him (Hebrews 9:22). Since we all sin, we could never be perfect; our blood is tainted because of our sin. So, on our own, we could never save ourselves. But because of God's love for us (John 3:16; Romans 5:8), God the Father (the first person of the Trinity) sent Jesus Christ the Son (the second person of the Trinity) to earth as a human (Galatians 4:4), but Jesus never stopped being God when He came to earth. He was born as a baby (Luke 1:30–33, 2:4–7, 21), He grew up (Luke 2:52), and lived as a man, but He never sinned. He was perfect (Hebrews 4:15). Jesus allowed sinful people to crucify Him on the Cross so that He could take the punishment for our sin (Hebrews 9:22). As a man, Jesus died physically. Since Jesus was God and sinless, He alone could provide the perfect blood sacrifice that God required as payment for our sin (2 Corinthians 5:21). After Jesus died on the Cross (Matthew 27:50), He was buried (Matthew 27:58–60), but on the third day He arose from the grave (Matthew 28:6). Many people saw Jesus after He was raised from the dead (Matthew 28:9, 16–17; Luke 24:13–51; 1 Corinthians 15:6). Jesus then returned to Heaven (Luke 24:51). But Jesus didn't want to leave us by ourselves (John 14:16–18), so He asked God the Father to send the Holy Spirit (the third person of the Trinity) to live inside believers who accept God's free gift

of salvation by asking Jesus to forgive them of their sin and trusting Him as their Lord and Savior (John 14:16–18; Ephesians 1:13–14). Through the ministry of the Holy Spirit, we can better understand the mysteries of God's Word, including the concept of the Trinity (1 Corinthians 2:14).

3. ABOUT CREATION

Creation is one of the most exciting and teachable doctrines found in the Bible. The very first verse of the Bible, Genesis 1:1, tells us that, "In the beginning, God created the Heavens and the earth." God is the Creator. He created everything. In the beginning, God was already there. God was not created; He has always existed. Genesis chapter 1 then tells us that God created the Heavens and the earth, the darkness and light, the sky, water, land, plants, trees, sun, moon, stars, fish, birds, and animals, all from nothing. God is all-knowing and all-powerful, so this was not hard for Him. God then took some dust from the ground (Genesis 2:7) and made a man in His own image and breathed the breath of life into him, and then made the woman from his side (Genesis 2:21-23). God made all of these things in six days and He saw that everything He made was good (Genesis 1:31). When the Bible says God created everything in six days, it means six literal, 24-hour days. Teach your child that the word used for "day" ("yôm ´ehäd") in Genesis 1:5 actually means a 24-hour day, not millions and millions of years. God can do anything, and creating everything in six days was not difficult for God. Help your child understand that everything created is by God's design (Romans 1:20). God specifically designed animals and plants in such a way as to help them grow and thrive in their environment. As children realize that God created them, we must explain to them that God has a unique design and purpose for their life as well. For more information and teaching ideas on the subject of creation, consider visiting answersingenesis.org and answersingenesis.org/kids.

4. ABOUT MANKIND

Many children today are being taught that they are the result of a "big bang," a random cosmic explosion in outer space! In essence, they are being taught that they are here on earth by accident. It is so important to teach children that they are not an accident, but instead, wonderful creations by God, lovingly designed and created for a unique purpose (Revelation 4:11; Isaiah 43:7). God tells us that each one of us is "fearfully and wonderfully made" (Psalm 139:14). God knows everything about every one of us (Psalm 139:1–16) because He is the one who "knitted" us together in our mother's womb (Psalm 139:13). These are some of the most important truths children can learn about themselves. Understanding about God's unique design for them is foundational because it helps them discover their created purpose in life, which is to bring glory to God (Isaiah 43:7; 1 Peter 2:9). The Bible also teaches that God created woman from man so that man would not be alone (Genesis 2:18). God designed and created man and woman for His glory (Matthew 5:16). Understanding that God created all of mankind, and that He loved us enough to send His only Son to pay for our sins (John 3:16), helps us value other people as God's unique creation as well.

5. ABOUT MARRIAGE

The Bible teaches that God created a woman (Eve) from the rib of a man (Adam), and then brought the woman to Adam so that the he would not be alone (Genesis 3:20–22). God had a specific creative order so that men and women would complement each other in their created purposes (Genesis 2:18; Ephesians 5:23–33). This is how marriage came to be. God designed marriage to be between one created man and one created woman (Genesis 2:4). Jesus clearly taught that marriage is between one created man and one

created woman (Matthew 19:4–5). The Bible teaches that a man should not be with another man, or a woman with another woman, in a romantic relationship (Leviticus 18:22; Romans 1:26–27). Knowing that we will one day give an account of our lives to God, we should follow His Word and not follow political correctness or cultural pressure. We should never be mean-spirited in proclaiming our beliefs. Instead, we should share what Gods Word says, in love, as truth from the Bible, calling them to repent of their sins knowing that God loves the person to whom we are talking, and that His Son, Jesus Christ, died for sinners (John 3:16). We should love them too!

6. ABOUT HOLINESS In the Old Testament, the Hebrew word for "holy" (qodesh), means "to be set apart from all others as sacred." In the New Testament, the Greek for "holy" is (hagios), which means blameless (without sin) and consecrated (set apart). God is holy (set apart) because He is greater than all others. God is without sin — this also sets Him apart from all others. In fact, God is so holy, that He cannot even look upon sin (Habakkuk 1:13). It is important that our children understand that holiness is the standard that will be used to judge everyone's life. God tells us to be holy, just as He is holy (Leviticus 11:45; 1 Peter 1:16). We grow up comparing ourselves with other people, but the Bible warns against doing that (2 Corinthians 10:12). Help your child understand that ultimately we will all be judged against God's perfect standard of holiness. John Calvin reasoned that, "Men are never duly touched and impressed with a conviction of their insignificance until they have contrasted themselves with the majesty of God." A proper understanding of God's holiness helps us put in perspective our sinfulness and need for salvation. Sin makes all of mankind unholy and imperfect before a holy God (Romans 3:23). We need to teach our children that because they have sinned, they can never attain holiness on their own (1 Samuel 2:2). Only through Jesus Christ can we be holy before God. Help them understand that Jesus, being part of the Trinity (see "About the Trinity"), is also God, and He is holy, too. Jesus died in order to pay for their sins, and if they trust in Jesus as their Lord and Savior, asking Him to forgive them of their sin, they can have their sins forgiven (John 3:16; 1 John 1:9). Jesus will take away our unrighteousness and give us His perfect righteousness in exchange (2 Corinthians 5:21).

7. ABOUT SATAN Children need to be taught that Satan (also called the devil and Lucifer) is real. The Bible teaches us that Satan was created; he has not always existed (Ezekiel 28:15). Unlike the cartoonish depictions of the devil with horns, a pointed tail, and a pitchfork, Satan was actually an angel who was kicked out of Heaven by God because of his pride (Ezekiel 28:17). Satan wanted to become greater than God (Isaiah 14:13–14). When God kicked him out of Heaven, one-third of Heaven's angels went with him (Revelation 12:4). Those fallen angels became demons who now follow and serve Satan (Revelation 12:9). Help your child understand that God is greater than Satan and his demons (Luke 10:17; 1 John 4:4). For now, God has allowed Satan to have some monitored authority in this world (2 Corinthians 4:4; Ephesians 2:2). Even though God has given Satan some authority, Satan must still answer to God (Job 1:6–12). We should never fear Satan, but we should have respect for his power and we should understand his strategies (2 Corinthians 2:11). Everything was created for God's glory, but Satan tries to use it for his own glory. He is an accuser of Christians (Revelation 12:10), he consistently tempts us to sin against God (Matthew 4:3; 1 Thessalonians 3:5), and he deceives us with lies (Genesis 3; 2 Corinthians 4:4; Revelation 20:3). However, Satan's end is certain. The Bible teaches that God has prepared an eternal lake of fire in Hell for the devil and his fallen angels (Revelation 20:10).

8. ABOUT SIN Sin is anything that doesn't please God or that breaks one of His laws (James 4:17; 1 John 3:4). We need to help our children understand that we are all guilty of sin before God (Romans 3:23). God gave us His perfect law, reflected in the Ten Commandments, to prove to us that we are all guilty of sin (Exodus 20:1–17). We have all broken God's perfect law (James 2:10). If we have ever taken something that did not belong to us, we are thieves in God's eyes (Exodus 20:19). If we have ever lied and not told the truth, we are liars in God's eyes (Exodus 20:16). If we have ever hated someone in our heart, we are murderers in God's eyes (1 John 3:15). The worst thing of all is that sin separates us from God. God is holy and cannot look upon sin (Habakkuk 1:13). Help your child understand that if God judges us on our sinfulness, He will find us all guilty, and because God is just and righteous, He must punish us for our sin. The punishment for sin is death without God, which means God must send us to Hell instead of Heaven (Revelation 20:11–15). Because we are sinful we cannot save ourselves. Jesus Christ, who is God the Son, came to earth and died for our sins (1 John 2:2). Jesus lived a perfect life; He never sinned. Instead, He paid the price for our sin (death) by dying in our place on the Cross. God required a perfect blood sacrifice to pay for sin, which we could never give because our own blood is tainted with sin. But Jesus' blood was without sin. He died for our sin, was buried, and then rose from the dead on the third day (Romans 10:9). He now offers us forgiveness of our sins. When we confess to God that we are sinners and turn from our sins by faith, Jesus Christ will forgive us of our sins (1 John 1:9) and become our Lord and Savior. We must also help our children understand that sin has affected and infected everyone who is born. Sin affects everything in a bad way! Romans 5:12 says, "Therefore, just as sin came into the world through one man [Adam], and death through sin, and so death spread to all men because all sinned." We have sickness and death because of sin (Genesis 2:15–17). Take a moment to name things that are bad in the world. Everything that is bad in the world is because of sin. Sin brings eventual death to everything and everyone it touches (Romans 6:23).

9. ABOUT JUDGMENT Because God is just and righteous, He must punish sin. God is the judge, and every person will stand before God one day and be judged (Revelation 20:11–15). There are two judgments mentioned in the Bible — the Judgment Seat of Christ, and the Great White Throne Judgment (2 Corinthians 5:10; Revelation 20:11). The Judgment Seat of Christ is for believers, those who have trusted Jesus Christ as their Lord and Savior. God will judge their lives and pronounce them innocent. Even though they have sinned, they will be found innocent because they accepted Jesus' substitutionary sacrifice (His death on the Cross) as payment for their sins. God will then give them rewards for their faithfulness (1 Corinthians 5:9–10), and they will spend eternity (forever) with God in a new Heaven and earth. The second judgment mentioned in the Bible is the Great White Throne judgment. It is for unbelievers, those who never trusted in Jesus. God will judge their sin and pronounce them guilty. The reason God will judge them guilty and punish them is because they did not believe in Jesus Christ as the sacrifice for their sins (John 3:16–18). God will give them their rightful punishment, which is spending eternity (forever) in Hell (Revelation 20:11–15).

10. ABOUT PUNISHMENT No one likes to talk about punishment, especially children. We can have hope when we discuss punishment with them because we know there is a way to avoid it. The Bible clearly teaches us that every person does things that do not please God or that break one of His laws (Romans 3:23). The Bible

calls this sin (see "About Sin"). While God is loving, and He does indeed love each one of us, He is also just and righteous. Because of this, He must punish sin. The punishment for sin is eternal (forever) death, separated from God, in Hell. Eternal death is different from physical death. Every person dies physically (Genesis 2:15–17; Hebrews 9:27), but everyone's soul will live forever in either Heaven or Hell. The Bible tells us "the wages of sin is death" (Romans 6:23). A wage is what we earn because of what we have done. When someone works a job all week long, the wage they earn for their work is a paycheck. What we earn for our sin is eternal death, separated from God, in Hell. That is what we all earn and deserve because of our sin. However, God made it possible for us to avoid Hell and experience eternal life by knowing God personally while we are here on earth (John 17:3) and then spending eternity with Him in Heaven when we die physically (John 3:16). God's gift of salvation, the forgiveness of our sins, is free to us because it was paid for by Jesus (Titus 3:5). Help your child understand that through Jesus' death, burial, and Resurrection, He purchased a place in Heaven for sinners, which He offers to them as a free gift (Ephesians 2:8–9). We accept that gift by faith, asking Jesus to forgive us of our sin and trusting Him as our Lord and Savior. For those who do not receive Jesus Christ's free gift of salvation, they will not only die physically when they take their last breath, but also eternally, and their souls will be in Hell forever as they suffer the punishment for their sin (Matthew 25:46; John 3:16–18). Help your child understand that God stands ready to forgive our sins and grant us eternal life through Jesus Christ (Romans 10:13).

II. ABOUT FORGIVENESS

There are two kinds of forgiveness. The first one is God's forgiveness; the second is our forgiveness toward others. God is the Creator (Genesis 1). He created the Heavens and the earth, and everything on the earth including people. God alone knows what is best for the people He created. When God created the first man and woman, Adam and Eve, He gave them the Garden of Eden as their home (Genesis 2:15). He also gave them one rule that they were to obey. He told them that they could eat fruit from any tree in the garden, except the tree of the knowledge of good and evil, and that if they ate from that tree, they would surely die (Genesis 2:16–17). What gave God the right to give them a rule to obey? He is the Creator. It was His earth, His garden, His fruit, His man, and His woman, His rule. Even though God had given them only one rule, Adam and Eve disobeyed God and broke His rule (Genesis 3:6). By breaking God's rule, they sinned, and when they did, sin entered into this world (Genesis 3:17). Because sin was in the world, God established more rules. What gave Him the right to do this? He is the Creator. He alone had the wisdom, the knowledge, the authority, and the right to establish the rules and laws for the people He created. So God established His perfect law, reflected in the Ten Commandments, which tells us how we should live (Exodus 20:1–17). The Ten Commandments prove to mankind that it is impossible for us to be perfect and sinless like God. We have all broken God's perfect law (James 2:10). Because we have broken God's law, we deserve to be punished (see "About Punishment"). The punishment we deserve for our sin is eternal (forever) death, separated from God, in Hell (Romans 6:23). The only thing that can pay for sin is a perfect blood sacrifice, which we could never give because our own blood is tainted with sin. However, because of God's love for us, His Son, Jesus, came to earth and lived a perfect life. He never sinned. Jesus died to pay for our sins (Romans 4:25) and was the perfect blood sacrifice that God required. After He died on the Cross and shed His sinless blood for our sins, He was buried, and then He rose from the dead on the third day (Romans 10:9). Jesus took our penalty for sin upon Himself when He died on the Cross (Isaiah 53:6). He now offers us forgiveness of our sins. Forgiveness comes through Jesus Christ alone (Acts 13:38). Only God can forgive our sin because it is His perfect law that we have broken. When we confess to God that we are sinners and turn from our sins by faith, Jesus Christ will forgive us of our sins (1 John 1:9) and become our Lord and Savior! When

God forgives our sins, He casts them as far as the east is from the west and remembers them no more (Psalm 103:12). Jesus died so we could be forgiven, and God wants to forgive us (2 Peter 3:9). However, we must recognize our need to be forgiven and confess our sins to God. Confessing is simply calling our sin what God calls it — wrong! We cannot pay for our sin; we can only receive the free gift of God's forgiveness. We receive forgiveness by faith, because of the grace of God (Ephesians 2:8–10).

The second kind of forgiveness belongs to us. Ultimately, only God can forgive sin, but we can choose not to hold something against another person when they have hurt us in some way. Our forgiveness is shown by refusing to have a bad attitude about a wrong committed against us (1 Peter 3:9; Romans 12:17). We choose not to hurt others in return for the wrong they have done to us (Matthew 5:38–40). When we forgive someone, we have confidence that God will take care of us and the situation in His perfect timing (Romans 12:19). We can still address the wrong with the person, but we must do it in a way that glorifies God (Colossians 3:17). Jesus gave us the perfect example of forgiveness when He forgave our sins. Now we must forgive others who sin against us (Colossians 3:13).

12. ABOUT THE FLOOD

The Bible tells us that because man's wickedness had become so great and there was so much sin on earth, God was grieved in His spirit (very sad) and decided He would destroy mankind with a worldwide flood (Genesis 6:5–8, 7:11). However, Noah found favor with God; he was a man who obeyed God and lived in a way that pleased God (Genesis 6:8–9). God was very specific in the directions He gave Noah about building the Ark. God told Noah what kind of wood to use in building the Ark, exactly how big to make it, and what types of food to put on the Ark (Genesis 6:10–23), because God alone knew what it would take to survive the Flood He was going to bring. Every living thing on the land perished during the Flood. Only what was on the Ark: two of every kind of creature (seven of some kinds) and Noah's family (Genesis 7:19–23). God promised He would never again destroy the earth by a flood and He gave us the rainbow that we sometimes see in the sky when it has been raining just to remind us of the promise He made (Genesis 9:8–17). The Bible's true account of the worldwide Flood and Noah's Ark is another wonderful opportunity to teach your child about salvation through Jesus Christ. Jesus called Himself the door of salvation (John 10:9). Just as Noah's family was saved from the Flood when they went through the door of the Ark, we can be saved from the coming judgment when we go through the door of salvation, Jesus Christ (Acts 4:12).

13. ABOUT PEOPLE GROUPS AND LANGUAGES

In Genesis 1 we learn how God created the Heavens and the earth and everything on the earth. God then tells us how He made the first man from the dust of the ground (Genesis 2:7) and named the man "Adam." God did not want Adam to be alone, so He made a woman and took the woman to Adam (Genesis 2:18–21). The woman's name was Eve. Adam and Eve were the first two people, the first married couple, who ever lived on earth. From this couple, everyone who ever lived was born (Genesis 3:20). Adam and Eve might not be their immediate parents, but Adam and Eve had children, then their children had children, then their children had children, then their children had children, and so on, and on, and on. Because of this, we know that there is only one true race of people on earth, the human race (Acts 17:26). Although there are many different people groups with different combinations of skin colors and facial features, and many different languages, every one of us comes from Adam's bloodline; we are all descendants of Adam (1 Corinthians 15:20). After the Flood, everyone on earth spoke the same language (Genesis 11:1). However, a

group of people decided that they would build a tower that reached up to Heaven. (Genesis 11:4). God was not pleased with this and chose to give them different languages so they couldn't understand each other (Genesis 11:7). The people then left in groups, by the language they spoke, to go live in different places on the earth (Genesis 11:8). God called the place where they were building the tower "Babel" (Genesis 11:9). As people moved into different locations and different climates, they carried their genetic traits with them, and those traits became the identifying characteristics of various people groups. We now see many different combinations of skin colors and facial features, even though we all come from the same bloodline of Adam, and God created all of mankind, each one of us, in His image (Genesis 1:26–27) (see "About Mankind").

14. ABOUT GOOD WORKS Many people think that if they are good enough, then they will go to Heaven. But God's requirement to get into Heaven is not being good, it is being perfect (Matthew 5:48), without sin, which none of us are. God makes it clear that it is not because of anything we have done that He forgives us (Ephesians 2:8–10; Titus 3:4–7), but because we have trusted in Jesus' death on the Cross as the payment for our sin, and asked Him to forgive us and have trusted Him as Lord and Savior. We are not saved by our good works, but we were created to do good works for God's glory (Matthew 5:16; Ephesians 2:10). If a person claims to be a Christian, but does not strive to live a good life, he or she might not be a Christian (James 2:14, 17, 20, 26). Just like an apple tree bears apples, the Bible tells us that we should be able to tell who is a Christian by the good things that they think, say, and do (Matthew 7:16–20). Before we become Christians, we do good deeds for personal reasons (Romans 8: 6–8). After we become Christians, we should do good deeds out of our thankfulness to God and to bring Him glory (Matthew 5:16). Sometimes children believe they are unloved when they do not obey. This is a great opportunity to reassure them of your unconditional love for them. More importantly, it is a wonderful time to tell them God loves us and desires that we worship Him! Help them understand that Jesus Christ knew that we would be sinners, but He still chose to come to earth and die for our sins (Romans 5:6–8). God knows that even after we become Christians we will not be perfect (Psalm 103:9–13), but He does expect us to be growing to be more like Christ (Romans 8:28–30; 2 Peter 3:18).

15. ABOUT GRACE Many people get the terms "mercy" and "grace" confused. To give "mercy" to someone means that you are not giving them what they deserve. To give "grace" to someone means that you are giving them what they do not deserve. Suppose your dad or mom tells you not to do something, but you disobey and do it anyway. When your parent finds out what you have done, he or she is not happy with you. You deserve to be punished because you disobeyed. But let's say that your parents tell you that they are not going to punish you this time. They have just given you their mercy (they did not give you what you deserved, which was punishment). What if they told you that instead of punishing you, they were going to take you to get your favorite meal and dessert for dinner? What they are now giving you is their grace. You deserve to be punished, but instead of punishing you, they give you something you do not deserve. Because we have done things that don't please God and have broken His Law (see "About Sin"), we deserve to be punished (see "About Punishment"). The punishment for sin is death without God (spending eternity in Hell — Romans 6:23), unless there is a perfect blood sacrifice (Hebrews 9:22). Since we all sin, we could never be perfect; our blood is tainted because of our sin. However, because of God's love for us, His Son, Jesus, came to earth and lived a perfect life; He never sinned. He died in our place and was the perfect blood sacrifice that God required to pay for our sin. After Jesus died on the Cross, He

was buried and then rose again on the third day. Through His death, burial, and Resurrection, He now offers to forgive us and to become our Lord and Savior. We did not work for or deserve what Jesus Christ did for us. We deserved to be punished for our sins. However, Jesus Christ took our punishment and made a way for our sins to be forgiven (Isaiah 53:5). When we confess to God that we are sinners and turn from our sins by faith, Jesus Christ will forgive us of our sins (1 John 1:9) and become our Lord and Savior! This is God's mercy — not giving us what we deserve. We will then know God personally while we are here on earth and also spend eternity with Him in Heaven when we die. This is God's grace — giving us what we do not deserve. But God's grace does not stop there. God also gives us everything we need to serve Him. Since God equips us through the power of the Holy Spirit to do what He desires, we can do "all things through Him" (Philippians 4:13; 2 Timothy 3:17). Sometimes it's easier to accept grace than it is to give or extend grace to others (1 Peter 4:10). Because God extended grace and forgiveness to us, even after we sinned against Him, it is important that we extend grace and forgiveness to other people who sin against us. God gives us grace to be saved from our sins and as we humble ourselves before Him, we will receive His grace (James 4:6), so that we can live our lives in a way that is pleasing to Him (2 Corinthians 12:9).

16. ABOUT JESUS CHRIST

Jesus Christ is the Son of God, the second person in the Holy Trinity; God the Father, God the Son, and God the Holy Spirit (Acts 5:3–4). The Trinity means that there is only one God, but that one God exists as three distinct persons (see "About the Trinity"). God reveals Himself to us through His Word. The Bible is the written Word of God to us (2 Timothy 3:16). Jesus is the Living Word of God (John 1:1, 14). The Bible tells us that God is spirit (John 4:24) and that He is invisible (Colossians 1:15), but it also tells us that Jesus is the image of God (Colossians 1:15) and the exact representation of God's being (Hebrews 1:3). We see who God is when we see Jesus. Although Jesus is God, He left Heaven and came to earth (John 1:1,14; Philippians 2:8). He was born as a baby (Luke 1:30–33, 2:4–7, 21). We recognize and celebrate His birth at Christmas. Jesus grew up (Luke 2:52) and lived as a man. He was tempted just like we are, but He never sinned (Matthew 4:1–11; Hebrews 4:15). Jesus lived a perfect, sinless life. God required a perfect blood sacrifice as the payment for our sins. Because Jesus was both God and man, He alone was qualified to pay for our sins (1 John 2:2; Romans 5:8; 2 Corinthians 5:21). As a human, Jesus had a physical body and could shed His blood for our sins. As God, Jesus was without sin and could pay for our sins. Salvation, being saved from the punishment we deserve because of our sins, is available only by asking Jesus Christ to forgive us of our sin and trusting Him as our Lord and Savior. That is why Jesus said, "I am the way, and the truth, and the life. No one comes to the Father except through me" (John 14:6). Jesus does not only want to be our Savior, to save us from our sins, we must also trust Him as our Lord and Savior. Jesus asked, "Why do you call me 'Lord, Lord,' and not do what I tell you?" (Luke 6:46). Lord means supreme in authority, the One who is in charge. Being the Creator, God knows what is best for the people He created, and Jesus proved His love for us when He died on the Cross. Jesus tells us that He came to give us an abundant life (John 10:10). We can trust Him to be our Lord and to lead us in a way that will be for God's glory and our good (Romans 8:28).

17. ABOUT THE RESURRECTION

After Jesus died on the Cross (Matthew 27:50), He was buried (Matthew 27:58–60), but on the third day He resurrected, which means He arose from the dead and became alive again (Matthew 28:6). Many people saw Jesus after He was raised from the dead (Matthew 28:9, 16–17; Luke 24:13–51; 1 Corinthians 15:6). Then Jesus returned to Heaven (Luke 24:51). Approximately 700 years before the Resurrection happened, God told the prophet Isaiah it was going to happen (Isaiah 53:3–5) and had him

write it down in the Old Testament. In the New Testament, when Jesus was asked by some of the Jewish people in Jerusalem what kind of sign He could show them to prove His authority, Jesus answered them, "Destroy this temple, and in three days I will raise it up" (John 2:18–20). The Jewish people thought Jesus was talking about the temple building where they worshiped that had taken 46 years to build, but the temple that Jesus was talking about was His body (John 2:21). The Bible goes on to tell us that after Jesus rose from the dead, His disciples recalled what He had said. Then they believed the Scripture and the words that Jesus had spoken (John 2:22). The Resurrection is a historical fact, witnessed by real people (Matthew 28:9, 16–17; Luke 24:13–51; 1 Corinthians 15:6) for 40 days before He was taken back to Heaven (Acts 1:3). The Apostle Paul considered the Resurrection of Jesus Christ of "first importance" in his teaching (1 Corinthians 15:3); it proved that God has power over death. Jesus' resurrection also proves that God the Father accepted the sacrifice of God the Son (Jesus) for sin. The Resurrection gives us great hope as we strive to live our lives for God's glory. When Jesus Christ arose from the grave, He provided, for all who would trust Him as Lord and Savior, eternal life that could not be taken away (1 Peter 1:3–4)! Not only does the Bible teach us about the Resurrection of Jesus, it also teaches that Jesus will return again for everyone who has trusted in Him (Matthew 24:7; Acts 1:11) (see "About the Rapture"). He is coming again! When Jesus returns, the Bible says the dead in Christ will be raised up first (resurrected), and those who remain and are alive, will be changed and receive a new and glorified body (1 Thessalonians 4:13–18). We need not fear death if Jesus Christ is our Lord and Savior (1 Corinthians 15:55–57).

18. ABOUT SALVATION Salvation means to be saved from something. Because we have sinned (see "About Sin"), we deserve to be punished. The punishment we deserve is eternal death, which is being separated from God, and spending eternity (forever) in Hell (see "About Punishment"). Salvation is being saved from that punishment. It is important that children understand that we are all sinners by nature, but God loves them and wants to forgive them of their sins. Every person is born with a sinful nature because we are all descendants of Adam who sinned (1 Corinthians 15:20). Adam's sin tainted all of creation with sin (Romans 5:12). Our sinfulness separates us from God who is holy and without sin. God also wants us to be holy and without sin (1 Peter 1:16). Because we are sinful in our nature, everything we do is tainted by sin, even our good works (Isaiah 64:6). Therefore, we cannot work our way back into a righteous and holy relationship with God. We need to be saved; we need a Savior because we cannot save ourselves. Salvation is a gift of God. We cannot earn it and we do not deserve it (Ephesians 2:8–9). God loves everyone (John 3:16). God also wants every one to be saved (1 Timothy 2:3–5). God already had a plan to provide salvation for sinners. Jesus Christ, who is God the Son, came to earth and took the form of a man (Philippians 2:6). Jesus Christ lived a sinless life and then gave His life to take the punishment for our sins (Matthew 20:28). Jesus died for sinners (John 3:16) and we have all "sinned and fallen short of the glory of God" (Romans 3:23), we must acknowledge Him as our Lord and Savior. We receive God's free gift of salvation by faith, believing that Jesus Christ died for your sins and arose on the third day. When we trust Jesus Christ as Lord and Savior, asking Him to forgive us of our sins, we are spiritually born again (John 3:1–8)! As with any gift, we cannot pay anything for it. If we do, it is no longer a gift; it is something we helped purchase. The Bible tells us that it is not because of anything we have done that God saves us, but it is because of His mercy (not giving us what we deserve) (Titus 3:4–7) and His grace (giving us what we do not deserve) (Ephesians 2:8–9) (see "About Grace"). There is only one way to be saved (Acts 4:11–12). We accept the gift of salvation by faith by asking Jesus Christ to forgive us of our sin and submitting to Him as our Lord and Savior.

19. ABOUT HELL We usually do not like to talk about things that are not pleasant or things that seem a bit scary. Hell is one of those things. But Hell is a real place, and we need to know and understand what God tells us about it in His written Word, the Bible (see "About the Bible"). God made Hell for Satan (also called the devil and Lucifer) and those who follow him (Matthew 25:41). Satan was an angel, created by God (Ezekiel 28:15). God kicked Satan out of Heaven, and when Satan left Heaven, one-third of Heaven's angels went with him (Revelation 12:4) and became demons who now follow and serve Satan (Revelation 12:9) (see "About Satan"). In the end, when Jesus returns back to earth (see "About the Resurrection"), He will defeat Satan and Satan will be thrown into Hell, where he will remain forever (Revelation 20:10). Hell is a horrible place. The Bible describes Hell as a lake of fire (Revelation 20:15) and a place of eternal (forever) punishment (Matthew 25:46). Those who are in Hell are shut out from the presence of God (2 Thessalonians 1:6, 9) and will be tormented day and night, forever and ever (Revelation 20:10). Sadly, Satan and his demons are not the only ones who will spend eternity in Hell. Everyone sins and deserves to go to Hell — that is the punishment for sin (see "About Sin" and "About Punishment"). The good news is that God loves us so much, that He made a way for us to avoid going to Hell through the forgiveness of our sins (see "About Sin" and "About Salvation"). Jesus Christ died for our sins and offers to save us from the punishment of Hell (Acts 4:12). Christians, those who have asked Jesus Christ to forgive them and have trusted Him as their Lord and Savior, do not have to fear Hell, because Christians will spend eternity in Heaven with God when they die. However, those who have not asked Jesus Christ to forgive them or trusted Him as their Lord and Savior will spend eternity in Hell (John 3:16,18, 36; 2 Thessalonians 1:6, 8–9; Revelation 20:15, 21:6–8). It is important to remember that only God knows what is in a person's heart. While the Bible tells us that we should be able to recognize those who are Christians by the good things that they think, say, and do (Matthew 7:16–20), we do not know their hearts. For this reason, we should pray for people and should try to help as many people as possible avoid going to Hell by telling them the good news of salvation through Jesus Christ before it is too late (Luke 16:19–31).

20. ABOUT THE BIBLE God reveals Himself to us through His Word. Jesus is the Living Word of God (John 1:1,14). The Bible is the written Word of God to us (2 Timothy 3:16). God chose the men He wanted to write down the actual words we read in the Bible, and God told each of those men the words He wanted them to write (2 Peter 1:20–21). God tells us that His Word is truth (John 17:17), His Word stands firm forever (Isaiah 40:8; 1 Peter 1:25), and His Word will not change (Matthew 5:18). We can trust that what we read in the Bible is truth, not just someone's opinion. Opinions can change, but truth never changes. The Bible teaches us what God wants us to know about Him. God uses His Word to teach us (Romans 15:4), to guide us (Psalm 119:105), to strengthen us (Matthew 4:4), to show us who we really are and who He wants us to be (James 1:23–25), and to encourage us (Romans 15:4). Unlike other books, the Bible is alive and is able to change us as we read and obey it (Hebrews 4:12). The Bible fully equips us to serve God (2 Timothy 3:17). We should study God's Word so we are prepared to respond to any situation in life (2 Timothy 2:15; 1 Peter 3:15). We must not try to change the Word of God to please ourselves (Revelations 22:18–19). The greatest thing the Bible reveals to us is the Gospel of Jesus Christ. It teaches us how we can have our sins forgiven and know God while we are here on earth (John 17:3), then live in Heaven with Him when we die. God's Word is a precious gift from God to us.

21. ABOUT THE HOLY SPIRIT The Holy Spirit is the third person in the Holy Trinity: God the Father, God the Son (Jesus Christ), and God the Holy Spirit (Acts 5:3–4). The Trinity means that there is only one God, but that one God exists as three distinct persons. (see "About the Trinity"). Not long before Jesus died on the Cross, He told His disciples that He was getting ready to return to Heaven. Jesus' 12 disciples had lived, traveled, and served with Him for three years. He had taught them and shown them, by His life, how they were supposed to live. Jesus told His disciples that even though He, God the Son, was leaving them physically, God the Father was going to send God the Holy Spirit to live with them forever (John 14:16–18). Jesus explained to them that the Holy Spirit would never leave them and He would always be with them because He would live inside of them (John 14:17). The Holy Spirit comes to live inside all people who ask Jesus Christ to forgive them of their sins and trust Him as their Lord and Savior (Ephesians 1:13–14), thus placing God's seal of ownership upon them (2 Corinthians 1:22). The Holy Spirit has the attributes of God because the Holy Spirit is God (see "About God"). The Holy Spirit is omnipresent, which means He is everywhere (Psalm 139:7–8). The Holy Spirit is omniscient, which means He knows everything (1 Corinthians 2:10–11). The Holy Spirit teaches us (John 14:26) and explains God's Word, the Bible to us (1 Corinthians 2:6–16). We should follow the leading of the Holy Spirit as He guides us in our hearts and minds (Ephesians 4:30). The Holy Spirit comforts and helps us as we walk through life (John 14:16). The Holy Spirit is our friend, and He helps us by representing us before God (Romans 8:26–27). The Holy Spirit convicts the world of sin, righteousness, and judgment (John 16:8), and He gives gifts to Christians to serve others (1 Corinthians 12:4–11).

22. ABOUT THE CHURCH When the Bible speaks of the Church, it is not talking about a building; it is talking about people. The Church is made up of people who have asked Jesus Christ to forgive them of their sins and have trusted Him as their Lord and Savior and now have the Holy Spirit living in them (Christians). The Bible tells us that Jesus is the Head of the Church, and the Church is His "body" (Ephesians 1:22–23). Just as the head directs all of the actions of a physical body, God intends for Jesus to direct all of the actions of the people who make up His Church body. Church was not man's idea; it was God's design, His plan. Jesus said He would build His Church (Matthew 16:18). God gives each one of us different abilities, which He intends for us to use for the good of all, to help build up His Church (1 Corinthians 12:1, 4–11; Ephesians 4:11–13). God tells us that as His Church, Christians are to continue to meet together, and when we do meet together we are to encourage each other (Hebrews 10:24–25). God does His work through local churches. Local churches are made up of saved and baptized members (Acts 2:41), who live near each other (1 Corinthians 1:2). Churches should teach God's Word and tell others about the good news that Jesus died for the sins of the world. The Church meets regularly to love and worship Jesus Christ and to learn more about Him (Acts 2:42), so they can go out from their gathering and live like Him (1 John 2:6). Local Bible-believing churches worship and serve God in specific communities (Acts 2:42–47). All churches, which are made up of baptised Christ followers who worship and serve God and observe the Communion (see About Communion), also make up what some people call the "universal Church." Every person who has ever asked Jesus Christ to forgive them of their sins and trusted Him as their Lord and Savior is a part of the universal Church (1 Corinthians 12:13).

23. ABOUT PRAYER Prayer is talking to God. God invites those who have asked Jesus Christ to forgive them of their sins and have trusted Him as Lord and Savior to come to Him in prayer (1 John 5:14). But how do you talk to God? What do you say to Him? We talk to God as if He were right there with us, because He is! God is omnipresent; He is everywhere (see "About God"). Jesus' disciples asked Him to teach them how to pray (Luke 11:1). Jesus then gave His disciples an example of how to pray (Luke 11:2–4). He wasn't telling them every time they pray they are to say those exact words, He was teaching them about God and about themselves. He first told them to call God "Father." When a person asks Jesus Christ to forgive them and to trust in Him as their Lord and Savior, they are born into the family of God. They were already born into the world with physical parents, but when they accept Jesus' gift of forgiveness, they are "born again" into God's family. God becomes their Heavenly Father, and they become God's child (John 1:12). So Jesus tells His disciples that they are to call God "Father" and to approach Him as His child (Luke 11:5–13). But unlike any human father, God is still holy and all knowing and all powerful and everywhere, etc. (see "About God"). So, while we can approach God as His child, we also need to remember who He is (Luke 11:2), giving Him the proper honor and respect that He deserves. Jesus goes on to teach His disciples that God cares about every aspect of our lives, our past (Luke 11:4), our presents (Luke 11:3), and our futures (Luke 11:4). When we are talking to God, we also need to remember to thank Him for who He is and for all He has done and continues to do for us (1 Thessalonians 5:18, Ephesians 5:20). Help your child understand that we can only go to God in prayer through His Son, Jesus Christ (John 14:6). God cannot look upon sin (Habakkuk 1:13), but Jesus Christ died for our sin and takes it away when we trust in Him (1 Peter 2:24). With Jesus as our Savior, we can go boldly to God in prayer (Hebrews 4:16). We should always pray instead of worrying about things (Philippians 4:6). When we pray, we must pray for things that please God and help us glorify Him. God does not answer our prayers when they are not in line with His Word and His will for our lives (James 4:2–3). We must make prayer a normal and consistent part of our day (James 1:6). When we pray and ask God for wisdom, He grants it so that we can make the right decisions (James 1:5).

24. ABOUT EVANGELISM Evangelism is telling others about the Gospel (1 Peter 3:15). *Gospel* means "good news," and sometimes just knowing the truth, even if it is not pleasant, is in reality good news. The Gospel is the truth that sin separates us from God, and that we have broken God's perfect law (Romans 3:23). God gave us His perfect law as reflected in the Ten Commandments to show us how we have broken His law (Galatians 3:24). For instance, the ninth commandment teaches that we should not lie. If we have ever told a lie, then we are liars. The eighth commandment teaches that we should not steal. If we have ever taken something that didn't belong to us, we have stolen and are therefore thieves. If we stand before God and He judges us based on His perfect law, we would be guilty, and when we die and stand before Him, God would have to judge us and send us to Hell (see About Punishment). But God so loved us that He sent His Son, Jesus Christ, to pay for our sins and provide salvation to everyone who believes in Him; that is the good news, the Gospel (1 Corinthians 15:1–11; John 3:16). Evangelism is telling that good news to others. In order for people to hear the good news about Jesus, someone has to tell them (Romans 10:13–14). In fact, Jesus told us to take the good news into "all the world" (Mark 16:15). God calls some people to be missionaries and share the Gospel with people who live in other places in the world, but every Christian is supposed to share the Gospel wherever he or she lives.

25. ABOUT BAPTISM Baptism is one of the two ordinances (practices) that Jesus gave to the local church to observe, the other being Communion or the Lord's Table (Matthew 28:19–20; 1 Corinthians 11:24–26). Many Christians understand baptism to be an outward picture of an inward decision that a person makes in his or her heart to trust Jesus Christ as his or her Lord and Savior. Baptism identifies us as Christ-followers. Baptism does not save you from your sin and it does not make you holier; it is the way we demonstrate to the world that we have faith in Jesus Christ as Lord and Savior. Baptism is also a matter of obedience for Christians. Baptism was not man's idea, but God's command. Before Jesus Christ went back to Heaven, He instructed all of His disciples to teach His Word (the Scriptures), make disciples, and then baptize those disciples (Matthew 28:19–20). Baptism illustrates the death, burial, and Resurrection of Jesus Christ. At the same time, it also illustrates our death to sin and our new life in Christ (Romans 6:4, 11; Colossians 2:12).

26. ABOUT COMMUNION Communion (or the Lord's Table) is one of the two ordinances (practices) given to the Church by Jesus Christ, the other being baptism (1 Corinthians 11:24–26; Matthew 28:19–20). Communion is a time to remember the death and victorious Resurrection of Jesus Christ. The bread represents the body of Jesus that He offered for us when He died for our sins. The cup represents the blood of Jesus that was shed for our sins. Before Jesus came to earth, the nation of Israel celebrated the Passover feast. The Passover was a reminder of the freeing of the Jews from slavery in Egypt — specifically, the night of God's tenth plague upon Egypt, when He sent His death angel to kill all the firstborn males of the land so that Pharaoh would finally free God's people who were in slavery to the Egyptians. The firstborn of God's people were saved because they placed the blood of a lamb on the doorposts of their houses. The death angel "passed over" the houses that had the blood (Exodus 12) on their doorposts, and their firstborn children were not killed. Jesus Christ came to earth to be our Passover lamb. He died and shed His blood for us so that we can have eternal life! Jesus told His disciples that as often as we celebrate Communion we would remember what He did for us on the Cross (1 Corinthians 11:23–26). We are supposed to observe Communion regularly until Jesus Christ returns (1 Corinthians 11:26). For Christians, Communion reminds us of the promise from Jesus Christ that He will return and deliver us. Just as God delivered the nation of Israel from physical slavery, God will deliver us from the slavery of sin through the blood of His Son (Luke 22:20). Communion is another outward picture of an inward decision that a person has already made in his or her heart to trust Jesus Christ as Lord and Savior. Only Christians, those who have already trusted in Jesus Christ, are to take part in Communion. Before taking Communion, we need to examine ourselves to make sure there is nothing we need to confess to Him.

27. ABOUT THE RETURN OF CHRIST Shortly before Jesus died on the Cross, He told His disciples that He was getting ready to return to Heaven (John 14:2). He also told them that He would come back to get them so that they could be with Him forever (John 14:3). After Jesus died on the Cross (Matthew 27:50), He was buried (Matthew 27:58–60), but on the third day He arose from the dead and became alive again (Matthew 28:6) (see "About the Resurrection"). For 40 days Jesus appeared to people with many convincing proofs that He was indeed alive (Acts 1:3). Some of these same people were with Jesus and saw Him when He was taken back up to Heaven (Acts 1:9). While they were still looking up into the sky, two angels appeared to them and told them

that Jesus, who they had just seen go up into Heaven, would come back in the same way they saw Him go into Heaven (Acts 1:10–11). The Bible makes it very clear that Jesus will come back again! After Jesus Christ returns He will judge Satan and sinners once and for all. He will take those who have asked Him to forgive them of their sins and have trusted Him as Lord and Savior to live with Him for eternity. God will restore all of creation back to its original state of perfection (Isaiah 65:17; Revelation 21:1).

28. ABOUT LEARNING GOD'S WORD

The Bible is the written Word of God to us (2 Timothy 3:16) (see "About the Bible"), so learning God's Word is very important! The Bible, God's Word, helps us to know who He is, what He is like, who He wants us to be, and how He wants us to live (2 Timothy 2:15, 3:16–17; James 1:22). God's Word teaches us right from wrong, it shows us when we are wrong, it tells us how we can get right, and it tells how we can keep on doing right (2 Timothy 3:16). God uses His Word to teach us and to encourage us. He also wants us to share with others what He has taught us, so they can know Him too. Before we read and study God's Word we should pray and ask God to help us to understand it (John 16:13; 1 Corinthians 2:14). We should also try to study complete passages of Scripture and not just one or two verses. That way we are able to understand exactly what God is saying. It's not easy to study and memorize verses, but when we store God's Word in our hearts and minds, we are able to learn, understand, and speak truth (2 Peter 1:3; Luke 6:45). Memorizing God's Word helps us not do the wrong things (Psalm 119:11). The purpose in studying God's Word is not just to become smart; knowledge alone makes us proud (1 Corinthians 8:1). We should study and memorize God's Word so that we can glorify Him with all we say and do (2 Timothy 2:15; 1 Corinthians 10:31).

29. ABOUT FAITH

Faith is believing in something we cannot see or touch (Hebrews 11:1). We cannot see air; it is invisible. But we breathe in air with every breath we take. Even though we cannot see air, we trust that it is going to be there when we need to take our next breath. Even though we cannot see air, we can see the evidence that air exists. When we take some of the air that we breathe in and blow out that air into a balloon, we can see the effects of the presence of the air as we watch the balloon get bigger. When we trust in what we cannot see, that is called faith. Believing in God takes faith (Hebrews 11:6). We cannot see God. The Bible tells us that God is spirit (John 4:24); He is invisible (Colossians 1:15). Even though we cannot see God, the world is filled with the evidence that God exists (Psalm 19:11). God is the One that makes sure the sun rises every day and sets every night (Job 38:12). He is the One that keeps the ocean from going any farther than it does when it reaches the shore (Job 38:8–11). God is the One who created people (Genesis 1:27, 2:7) and designed how all of the different parts of the body would work together (Psalm 139:13) (see "About God" and "About Mankind"). We especially need faith to trust in God and all that He has written in the Bible. When we understand that Jesus Christ left Heaven and came to earth to take the punishment we deserve because we have sinned and broken God's perfect law, and that those who ask Jesus Christ to forgive them of their sin and become their Lord and Savior are saved from the punishment they earned because of their sins, we have a faith decision to make. Will we trust in Jesus Christ and His death on the Cross to save us from the penalty we deserve? Those who make the decision to ask Jesus to forgive them and trust in Him as their Lord and Savior, make that decision by faith. We are saved by God's grace (see "About Grace") through faith, trusting in what we cannot see and did not witness personally (Ephesians 2:8). Once we have received salvation, faith also helps us to please God. If we do not have faith, we cannot please God (Hebrews

11:6). So how do we get faith? Faith is a gift from God (Ephesians 2:8–9). When we receive Jesus Christ as our Lord and Savior, God gives us the gift of faith to believe. God gives us faith as we read and listen to His Word (Romans 10:17). God rewards us when we live by faith and not simply by sight (Hebrews 11:6; Luke 7:50). Faith allows us to accomplish great and small things for the glory of God (Matthew 17:20). Faith ultimately helps us gain peace with God and ourselves (Romans 5:1). There are many examples given in the Bible of those who have lived by faith (Hebrews 11).

30. ABOUT HEAVEN

Heaven is a real place! Heaven is where God lives (Luke 11:2; Revelation 21:3). God is everywhere (see "About God"), but Heaven is where God reigns over all of creation (Psalm 103:19). Heaven is also where Jesus is. Jesus was in Heaven with God in the beginning (John 1:1,14), but He came to earth to do the one thing He couldn't do for us in Heaven, which was die on the Cross to take the punishment for our sin (Matthew 27:32–50) (see "About Sin" and "About Punishment"). Jesus was then buried (Matthew 27:58–60), but on the third day, He arose from the dead and became alive again (Matthew 28:6) (see "About the Resurrection"). Forty days later (Acts 1:3), Jesus was taken back up to Heaven (Acts 1:9), which is where He is today. Heaven is also where Christians, those who have asked Jesus to forgive them and have trusted Him as their Lord and Savior, will spend eternity (forever) when they die (John 14:2–3). We know that Heaven is beautiful! The Bible tells us that the gates in Heaven are made of pearls and the street in Heaven is made of gold (Revelation 21:21). There is a great, high wall in Heaven that has 12 foundations (Revelation 21:14) that are decorated with every kind of precious stone (Revelation 21:19) that are different colors. There is a river as clear as crystal that flows down the middle of the city (Revelation 22:1–2). In Heaven, there will be no more night (Revelation 22:5). Heaven does not need the light of a lamp or the light of the sun or the moon to shine on, because the glory of God gives it light (Revelation 21:11,23). In Heaven, there will be no more death, or mourning, or crying, or pain (Revelation 21:4). What God tells us about Heaven is wonderful; however, He also tells us that no one has ever seen or heard or even imagined what He has prepared for those who love Him (1 Corinthians 2:9)!

THE AUTHOR

Jeff Davenport is a pastor in Covington, Kentucky, where he enjoys communicating God's Word and encouraging God's people through writing and teaching. He and his wife, Beth, have three adult children and several grandchildren, who call them Poppie and Grammie!

THE ILLUSTRATOR

Bill Looney is a talented artist and musician, educated at the University of Texas at Arlington and the Dallas Art Institute. He entered the arena of professional commercial art and illustration in the early '70s. Most recently, Bill's artwork has been published in such books as *The Flood of Noah, Giants: Legends & Lore of Goliaths,* and *Dragons: Legends & Lore of Dinosaurs.*

ENDORSEMENTS

"Great format with great questions to help inculcate God's truths to young, developing minds. Children learn best when information is presented in the context of ideas with which they are familiar. I feel strongly that this book will help children to hide His Word in their hearts so that they will more strongly serve Him."

—W. Mark Posey, PhD.,
Associate Professor of Clinical Pediatrics at the
University of South Carolina School of Medicine
(Pediatric Psychologist)

ACKNOWLEDGMENTS

No book is ever written by a single person. Instead, it is a collaboration of many who share a common goal. In this case, the goal was to follow the precept and promise of Proverbs 22:6 and help equip parents and teachers to effectively, *"Train up a child in the way they should go…"* so that, *"when they are old they will not depart from it."*

First and foremost, I want to acknowledge my Lord and Savior Jesus Christ whose unmatched sacrifice of love and grace makes the message of this book a wonderful reality! Without Him, we have nothing about which to write or celebrate.

To my wife, Beth, who so lovingly edits both my writing and my life. Her faithful commitment, constant encouragement, and abiding love provided the fuel for this project.

To my friends at Answers in Genesis: Ken Ham, Mark Looy, and many others on their team who daily contend for the faith and believed in the importance and content of this book.

To my Administrative Assistant, Karen Giger, for taking her personal time to pour over the manuscript and make it better. Your love for Christ and His Word are evident.

To my many family members and friends who have always encouraged me to put "pen to paper," or in this case, "fingers to keyboard!" Our children by birth and marriage: Lauren, Kyle, Nathan, Suzanna, and Mitchell. Our grandchildren, Laelle, Karys, and Kreed (and all who will follow them); they were the original motivation to write this book. My mom, Patty, who first followed Christ and then introduced her three sons (Mike, Jeff, and Clif) to Him. My dad, Sonny, who taught me the importance of integrity and laughter. My wife's mother, Mary, I'm blessed daily by the example you set for Beth! Our lifelong friends, Gerry and Belinda, you have always reminded us of what's possible with God.

To my Leadership Team at Calvary… you guys make ministry a joy! Also to the members and fellow-laborers at Calvary, Mamre, Agape, and Northside… God used you all to mold me. Thank you for your partnership and kingdom attitude. You looked beyond the walls of the church and encouraged me to do the same.

To the extreme team at New Leaf! Tim Dudley sees what can be! Thank you for your confidence and encouragement. You and your team's commitment to biblical accuracy and above all, the glory of God, continues to propel the rich history of New Leaf and Master Books forward! And finally, to Bill Looney, you brought the message of this book to life with color and creativity!